THE POWER OF THE
PENNY

ABRAHAM LINCOLN INSPIRES A NATION

Written & Created by Elaina Redmond

Illustrated by Scott Stewart

For information regarding permission write to: Spencer Publishing P.O. Box 351492, 1270 S. Alfred St., Los Angeles, CA 90035

or email: powerofthepenny@aol.com

First Edition 2009

Many thanks to Chadwick J. Coleman for your heroic help!
Thank you to sweet and insightful Anna Li Cortese.

Layout design by Chadwick J. Coleman

Printed in Hong Kong

Printed with soy based ink

www.thepowerofthepenny.com

The illustrations were created with pencils and inks. Color was applied in Adobe Photoshop.

ISBN: 978-09815515-0-0

Dedication

To my beautiful Mother Maria: Thank you for being my Magical Muse!

To the children of the United States and the World:
This book is my gift to you!
So tag you are it! As the next generation creating this world,
always remember Abraham Lincoln and the penny are here to
inspire you on your wonderous life path.

Elaina Redmond

The Power of the Penny

Take a look at the penny we forget to see,
A symbol for all, of the hero we struggle to be.

It's worth the least, in the worldly material sense,
But holds deepest treasures within its true essence.

As you peer take note of the word liberty,
The value that lets us practice spiritually.

And written on top, is a message to us,
We are not alone, our life is "In God We Trust."

But what separates this coin from its brothers,
Is the man on the front, who is like no other.

His name is Lincoln, but became Honest Abe,
As he taught us the true meaning of becoming self made.

Now turn over the penny & read "E Pluribus Unum,"
A latin phrase meaning "Out of Many, One."

Out of many you can be "One" like Lincoln,
To travel the path of a hero, living life with inspiration.

So let the penny be your guide, any moment of the day,
To inspire you with love & truth, in creating your way.

Have you ever walked by a penny without paying attention to it?

The penny may be small, but it's a symbol of the positive values you can use to live the path of a hero while overcoming your scary dragons of fear.

Do you want to be a Hero?

When you see a penny pick it up and appreciate its incredible worth. The penny teaches us that no matter how big the world around us is or how small we might feel, each of us can make a difference everyday.

Are you ready to learn more about the penny and its powerful ways?

This way to be a HERO!

The Path

The penny is worth the least in the worldly material sense, but holds deepest treasures within its true essence.

Like the penny, you hold special inner qualities that are needed in this nation.
No matter who you are, you too can inspire others with love and care, just by your participation.

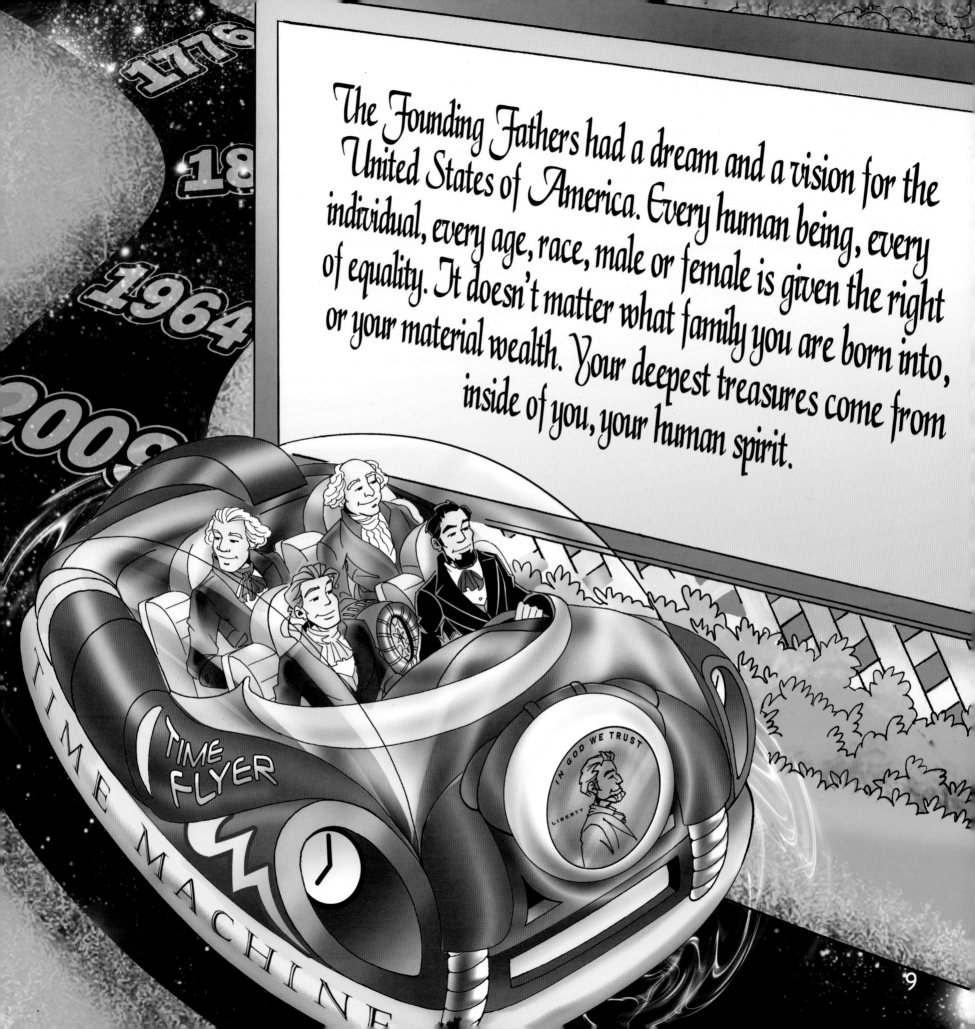

The Founding Fathers had a dream and a vision for the United States of America. Every human being, every individual, every age, race, male or female is given the right of equality. It doesn't matter what family you are born into, or your material wealth. Your deepest treasures come from inside of you, your human spirit.

9

As you peer at the penny
take note of the word "Liberty."

This is the value that lets us
practice spiritually.

Look back into history...

In 1776, Thomas Jefferson, a Founding Father of this Republic, wrote the Declaration of Independence. This extraordinary vision guides our country in allowing every citizen to count with a fundamental right to liberty. This includes YOU.

Mr. Jefferson believed in nature's God, but he wanted every person to have the right to practice, in peace, his or her own view of God, religion and spirituality. Liberty written on the penny shares with us the power of this everyday value.

This idea makes our country *"America the Beautiful,"* because all people and their beliefs are honored.

Written on top, is a message to us,
We are not alone, our life is "In God We Trust."

12

The penny symbolizes faith.

The Founding Fathers used faith in the human spirit to create a country unlike any other. They envisioned this country as a Great Experiment, birthing new values for its citizens, guided by Divine Providence. No other country in the history of the world had bestowed the rights and values of life, liberty and the pursuit of happiness to all its citizens living within its lands.

Let the penny inspire trust in the unseen divine forces, the laws of nature and your human spirit to live out the possibility of creating greatness in the everyday.

13

WHAT SEPARATES THIS COIN
FROM ITS BROTHERS,

IS THE MAN ON THE FRONT,
WHO IS LIKE NO OTHER.

ABRAHAM LINCOLN LED THE BIGGEST AND BLOODIEST CHALLENGE IN UNITED STATES HISTORY; THE CIVIL WAR. THE NATION WAS DIVIDED AND IN A DEEP CRISIS. THE NORTH AND SOUTH VIOLENTLY DISAGREED OVER SLAVERY, STATES' RIGHTS AND ECONOMICS. PRESIDENT LINCOLN'S GOAL WAS TO PRESERVE THE UNION AND BUILD ONE STRONG COUNTRY.

ABE LINCOLN BROUGHT TO LIFE THE WRITTEN VISION OF THE FOUNDING FATHERS. HE BELIEVED JUSTICE, EQUALITY AND LIBERTY WERE FOR ALL PEOPLE OF ALL COLORS. IN 1863, AS THE CIVIL WAR RAGED ON INTO ITS THIRD YEAR, LINCOLN BOLDLY DECLARED THE

Emancipation Proclamation

TO END SLAVERY. SADLY, PRESIDENT LINCOLN WAS ASSASSINATED A YEAR LATER, BUT ALL THAT HE STOOD FOR, LIVES ON.

ABRAHAM LINCOLN'S CHARACTER AND HIS ABILITY TO WRITE AND SPEAK GAVE HIM THE STRENGTH TO FREE THE SLAVES AND SAVE THE NATION. HE IS A TRUE AMERICAN HERO.

His name is Lincoln, but became *Honest Abe*, as he taught us the true meaning of becoming self made.

Mr. Lincoln developed personal style by building character and going the extra mile. Everyone knew him as honest, decent, trustworthy and kind. Even his enemies agreed Lincoln's character was to be admired.

Abraham Lincoln deeply contemplated life, human nature and even called upon divine inspiration to guide him. Honest Abe used his power to affirm human values even when he was unpopular.

ABRAHAM LINCOLN was nicknamed HONEST ABE.

Abe developed his character over many years. As a shopkeeper, he once miscalculated and overcharged a woman. He then walked a mile to her house and returned the money. Abe had very little formal education, but he chose to educate himself. He read books and applied what he learned. He also chose to make money without hurting or taking advantage of people less fortunate. When he was a country lawyer, Lincoln even charged a lesser fee for people with less money.

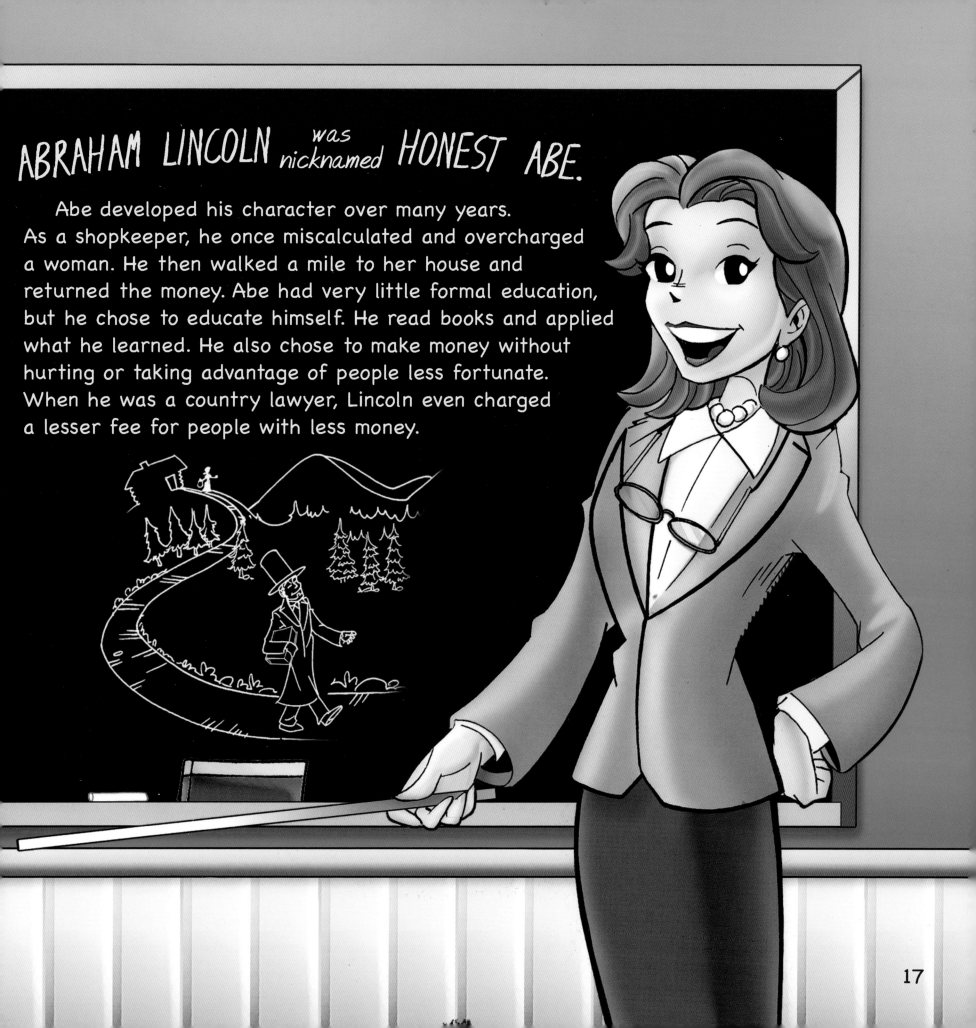

Now turn over your penny and read the Latin words, "E Pluribus Unum," meaning "Out of Many, One."

You can be the "One" out of many, like Honest Abe to live the path of a hero making a difference each day.

As you live this path of inspiration and care,

You will be unique & special in how you share.

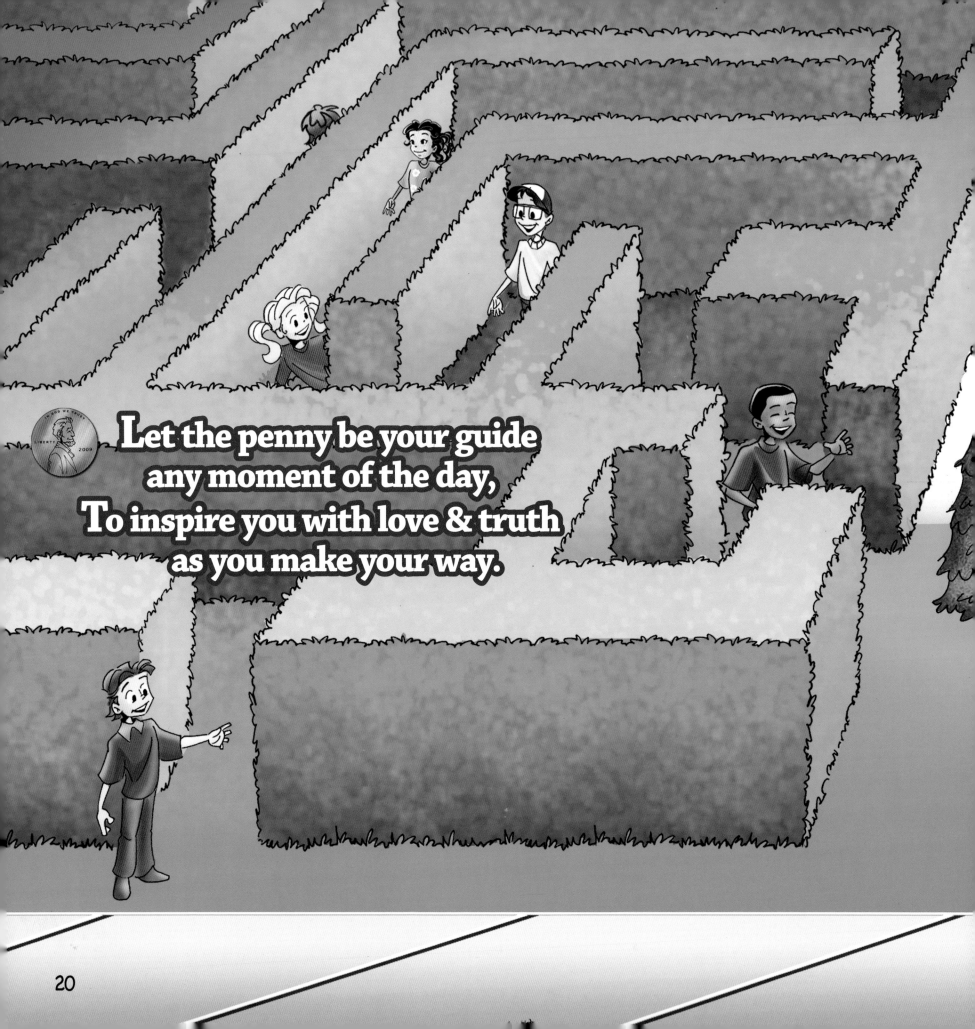

Let the penny be your guide
any moment of the day,
To inspire you with love & truth
as you make your way.

Now you know the Lincoln penny is more than just a coin.

The Power of the Penny is yours anytime or anywhere at home, on the street or in a store. Pick up the penny and admire its worthiness and heroic message.

As a symbol of the positive values of this great nation, the penny reminds you to be like Honest Abe, a hero & inspiration.

When you see the penny, think of it as a messenger of HOPE! Let it inspire possibility as you travel a Hero's journey; to build character, conquer fear and create your dreams.

The Power of the Penny
holds special instructions,

For you to use in building
your life's construction!

You have arrived at
the *Penny Practice*.

Now it is up to you to take action in how you live!

These upcoming practices put into action the positive values of this great nation. They include ideas and activities for you to think about and do.

The practices will also help you be a hero in everyday life as you build your character like Lincoln.

So are you ready to practice the *"The Power of the Penny?"*

Here we go...

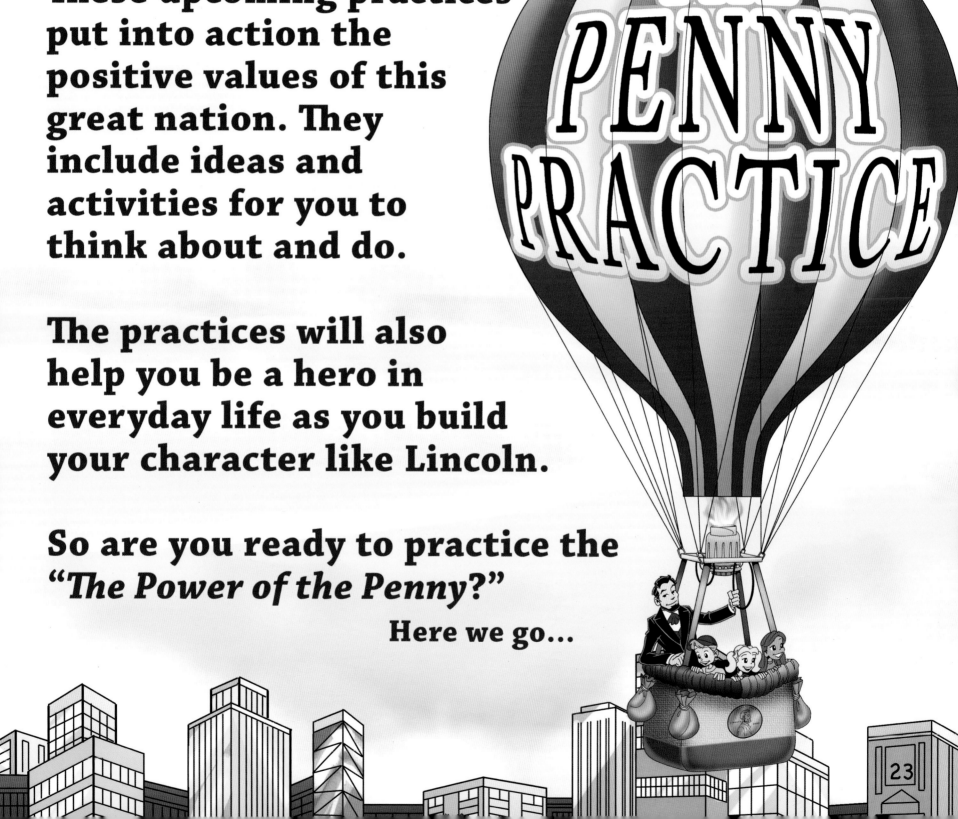

THE PENNY PRACTICE

Walk your path of life building character like Lincoln & practice The Power of the Penny.

Activities

1. Say three reasons why you think you are special and what you like most about yourself.

2. Pick a new skill or talent you would like to develop & begin learning it.

Sometimes learning is hard, so remember to practice persistence!

Develop yourself to be your best and stand strong as "One" from many.

You have the freedom to choose how to live your life

Be glad for the vision of the Founding Fathers, still a gift to us today. Like Lincoln who used this vision, we too can be inspired to make a better tomorrow.

Learn and grow to shape and show how your choices help this world and this nation stand as a force for positive creation.

Activities

1. What choices can you make today that will build you into your best self?

2. Ask your parents or guardian to take you to see a historical site in your local area or look up a historical site on the internet and imagine yourself there. What inspiring idea from this place can you apply to your own daily life?

Be like Abe Lincoln

Character is felt by all who meet you
while you're living on earth.

Character is seen through your actions,
and determines real value and worth.

Abe Lincoln came from humble beginnings. He was born in a log cabin in Kentucky and sadly lost his mother at age 9. Abe always tried to do his best during his life. He developed himself using self education and persistence.

Develop your gifts and talents no matter what your life circumstances are! Build your character like Lincoln and become a better you, strong in who you are. If you are unhappy, sad or mad, practice using positive actions. Overcome feeling bad by learning to be glad.

Activity/Practice

1. Why do you like Abe Lincoln? Describe a character trait he has and think about how you can practice it. Here are a few traits Abe is known for; courage, persistence, honesty, kindness, speaking well and writing clearly.

2. Go get paper and a pencil, markers or some crayons. Now draw an image of you and be your own biggest fan. What makes you strong and allows you to be your best? Draw your ideas & how you make a difference to inspire the rest.

No matter the outcome, heads or tails, win or lose, remember your attitude and actions are what you choose.

So practice living on the side of

KINDNESS

Abe Lincoln acted with kindness throughout his life.

He liked helping people while valuing fairness. He cared for family, friends and foes. He even forgave his enemies.

Take Action!

Do, feel, act and be, using kindness and honesty with yourself and those around you.

Activities/Practices

1. Have you been mean, a bully, or hurt someone's feelings? If so, go up to the person & say you're sorry.

2. If your feelings have been hurt or you are upset with someone, practice telling this person the truth, while still being nice.

3. Make a practice of being kind, caring and loving to others in everyday interactions. When making a decision, say to yourself: "What is the kindest action I can take?"

Practice Honesty with yourself

Honest Abe took the time to listen, to his mind, heart, body and soul. He was dedicated to self education and honesty, this is how he was able to grow.

So stand at attention and stand tall, to your pains and passions. These are your guides and tools to live in a heroic and honest fashion.

It's easy to say "tell the truth," but sometimes it is hard to do. If this happens to you, practice being courageous like Abraham Lincoln did.

PAIN PASSION

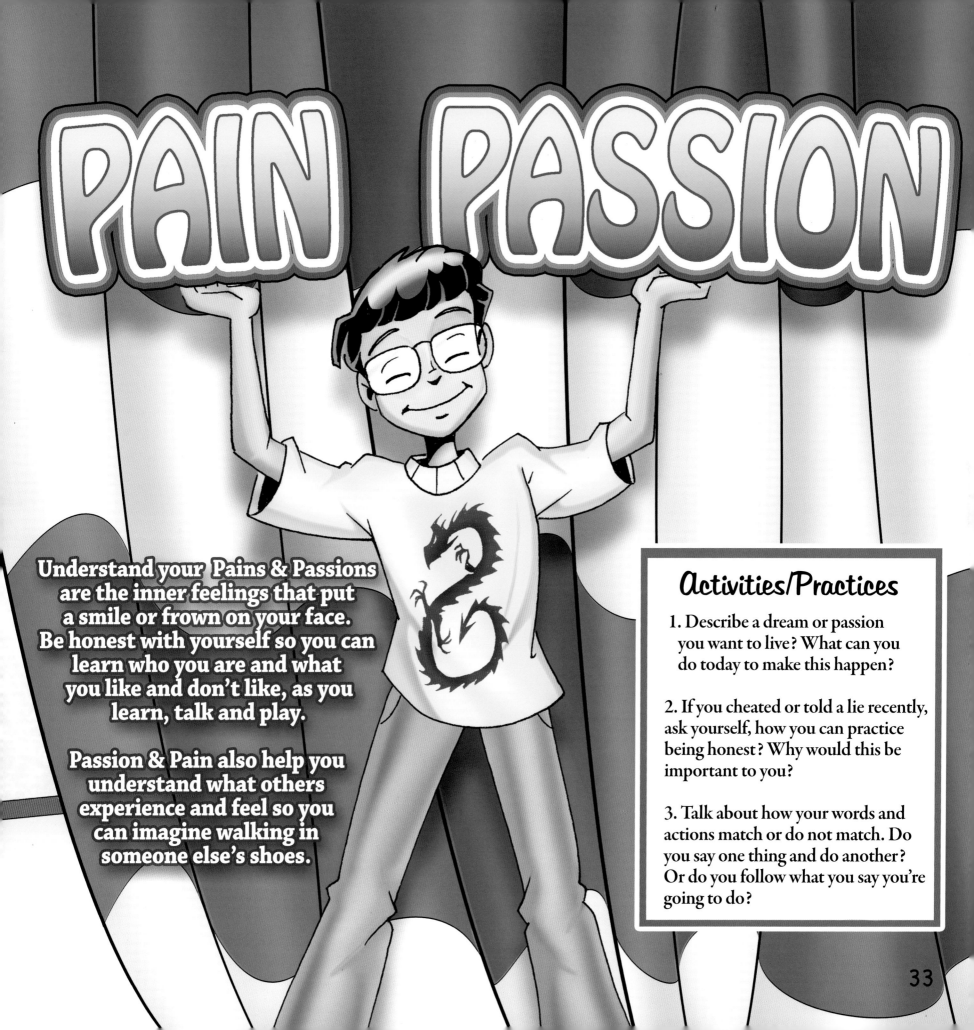

Understand your Pains & Passions are the inner feelings that put a smile or frown on your face. Be honest with yourself so you can learn who you are and what you like and don't like, as you learn, talk and play.

Passion & Pain also help you understand what others experience and feel so you can imagine walking in someone else's shoes.

Activities/Practices

1. Describe a dream or passion you want to live? What can you do today to make this happen?

2. If you cheated or told a lie recently, ask yourself, how you can practice being honest? Why would this be important to you?

3. Talk about how your words and actions match or do not match. Do you say one thing and do another? Or do you follow what you say you're going to do?

Practice Money Wisdom

Whether money is plentiful or not always use lots of imagination,

To move the biggest mountains with love, care and inspiration!

Activity/Practice

1. Have your parents or guardian explain the importance of using money wisely.

2. Instead of spending all your money today put your money in a safe place and save up for something special.

Even if you've got just
a penny in your pocket
remember building character,
like Lincoln, is a ticket to
doing good in the world.

And when money does flow,
allow your hard earned
pennies to be moved by the
thoughts of your heart.

You never know where your
human heart will take you,
so go ahead, listen to it
and let it surprise you!

Happiness will follow your heart's lead!

Pursue Happiness!

Happiness is in the details of living.
It's an exchange of love & care by receiving & giving.

Happiness is a challenge and a choice,
experienced by living your authentic inner voice.

Lincoln found qualities inside himself to bring happiness to others. His folksy passion and melancholy pain gave him the strength to unite a country, making it possible for you to pursue happiness.

Be a diligent detective and discover what makes you happy. Clear the clutter of chaos and confusion from your mind and heart and appreciate every day as a new start.

Activities

1. Name two things that make you unhappy or fearful and say how you can change them.

2. Look at the current events in your neighborhood. What can you do to bring happiness to a person, animal or place? Try one of the following: make a card & deliver it, visit someone & sing to them, volunteer your time, or imagine another idea.

Activity

Now its your turn to write a poem about *The Power of the Penny*.
Imagine Lincoln here with you, still a friend to many.

Think about the positive values the penny stands for,
& now let your pen or pencil soar.

When you are done writing, feel proud,
& share your poem with others, reading it aloud.

This book may be ending, yes it's true,
but the penny's inspiration has just begun for you.

The time has come for you to live Penny Power!
It's your guide on the hero's path to grow & flower.

Becoming a Hero can take work, & that is ok.
As you build character, like Lincoln, you must be brave.

The Founding Fathers & Lincoln are counting on you,
to live their American vision and positive values, too.

It's your turn to pursue happiness, dreams and liberty,
while practicing kindness, money wisdom and honesty.

Go now and share the poem, The Power of the Penny.
Go tell neighbors, friends and family.

As you share the power of the Everyday Penny,
You will bring love, beauty and inspiration to many.